Around Tamworth

IN OLD PHOTOGRAPHS

The 1913 Tamworth Millenary Celebrations. Mrs H. Argyle, wife of one of the town's leading solicitors, portrays Aethelflaeda, Lady of the Mercians, who regained Tamworth from the Danelaw in AD 913. The young Richard Ford played Athelstan, Aethelfaeda's nephew, who succeeded his father Edward as king of a united England.

Around Tamworth

IN OLD PHOTOGRAPHS

RICHARD SULIMA

Alan Sutton Publishing Limited
Phoenix Mill · Far Thrupp · Stroud
Gloucestershire · GL5 2BU

TAMWORTH BOROUGH COUNCIL

First published 1994
Reprinted 1995

British Library Cataloguing in Publication Data.
A catalogue record for this book is available from the British Library.

ISBN 0-7509-0621-9

Typeset in 9/10 Sabon.
Typesetting and origination by
Alan Sutton Publishing Limited.
Printed in Great Britain by
Ebenezer Baylis, Worcester.

Tamworth police force at the rear of Church Street police station (now the social services offices), 1933–4. Front row, left to right: PC Kemp, Sgt Thomas W. Bickley, Inspector Brookes, the mayor, Mr A.H. Weale, Sgt ?, PC Chinnock, PC Baines. Back row: PC George Parkes, PC 'Jock' Ferguson, Sgt ?, Sgt Shelton, PC Len Shaw, 'George' Frederick W.H. Turner. All are wearing their 'best uniform' with black braid on cuffs and the superb shako caps, which were withdrawn a few years later. The mayor of the time was the town's longest-serving professional photographer. He and his father, C.E. Weale, provided many of the historic photographs in this collection.

Contents

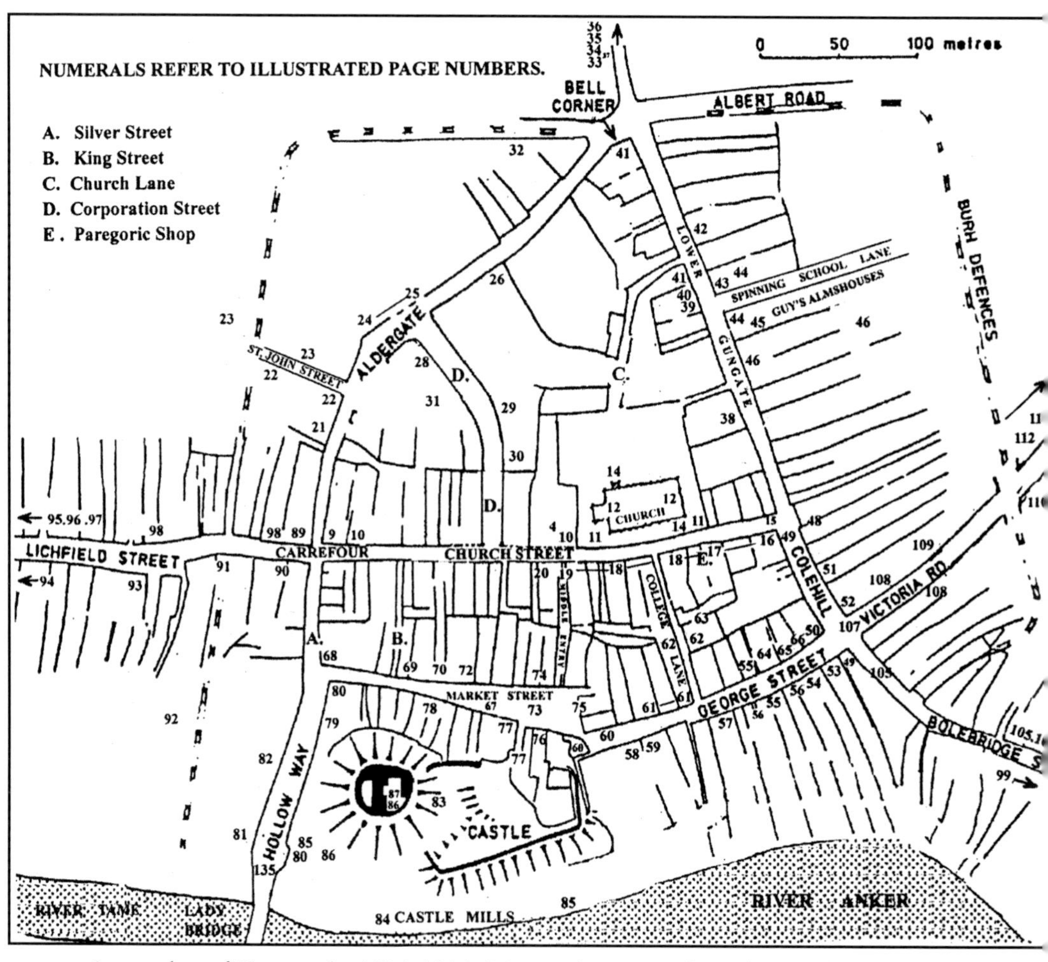

Street plan of Tamworth, 1884–1904. Map and property boundaries adapted by kind permission of R. Meeson.

Introduction

The history of the ancient Saxon and Medieval Burgh of Tamworth has been well recorded in Palmer's *History of the Town and Castle of Tamworth* (1845) and H. Wood's *Borough by Prescription (1958)*.

This book is not intended solely as a history book. Instead, the photographic image records the recent past in a more immediate and vivid way than the printed word alone. The book can be used by Tamworthians and tourists alike as a guide to the principal streets of this ancient borough. The photographs are in consecutive order wherever possible, progressing from one side of the street to the other.

We start from the crossroads at the west end of Church Street and travel along the north side to the church, then to the junction with Colehill and retrace our steps past the vanished Paregoric Shop and Middle Entry along the south side, returning to the old Carrefour crossroads at the western end. Aldergate, Corporation Street, Lower Gungate, George and Market Streets have been treated in the same manner. Others, such as Victoria Road, have, because of their nature, been broken into sections and travel is in one direction.

Thus the preceding and succeeding photographs will help to locate in their original position buildings which have vanished, been altered, or been replaced in relation to the surviving buildings. Where possible, people, events and vehicles have been chosen for the foreground while the street sequence has been retained in the background.

Tamworth still retains a range of prestigious historic buildings: St Editha's Church, the Castle, the Moat House and Guy's Town Hall. All are depicted in E.B. Hamel's *Illustrations of Tamworth* (1829). This is the earliest comprehensive series of views of Tamworth in the pre-photographic age, presenting historical detail not available elsewhere. Hamel's late Georgian street views are particularly useful, especially Market Street. They all show small-scale late medieval buildings, many refaced with brick and almost indistinguishable from their late eighteenth- and nineteenth-century neighbours.

The introduction of the railways and the rising prosperity of the Victorian period saw a great deal of building activity, still mainly small scale, but in keeping with earlier styles, and this is well illustrated here.

The first few photographs of Tamworth start to appear in the 1850s and '60s, but it is not until the late 1870s and '80s that photographs of the town, mainly by W. Hulland and C.E. Weale, begin to appear in any number.

The later Victorian and Edwardian periods saw civic zeal and pride at their zenith, with the creation of public amenity buildings, both larger in size and more richly ornamented than before. There were two leading private donors in the late nineteenth century. The vicar, Revd William MacGregor, who funded the building of the Church Street Baths and Institute, also built Hopwas

Church and the Cottage Hospital; and Mrs Hutton of Dosthill Hall paid for the extension to the hospital and the Hutton Fountain.

In the same period public subscription paid for the building of the 1889 Assembly Rooms, and the purchase of Tamworth Castle in 1897. The Carnegie Library was added in 1905. Its façade is typical of the period, as is the sparsely decorated 1904 Union Workhouse, which later became St Editha's Hospital. The other great influence, which transformed the town socially, economically and architecturally, was the Tamworth Co-operative Society.

Few of Tamworth's civic and public occasions were photographed before 1914. The major events included the large-scale street parties held in Market Street to mark Queen Victoria's Diamond Jubilee and the official opening of the borough's newly acquired Castle Museum in 1899.

The 1913 Millenary Celebrations commemorating Aethelflaeda's refounding of Tamworth in AD 913, with its seven-part open-air pageant and other public entertainment, drew both the crowds and the photographers from neighbouring districts. Although a series of over fifty postcards was originally issued, the museum's collection only contains a few, some of which are included here.

For general entertainment the town benefited greatly from the addition of two cinemas, both in George Street. Thornburn's first Palace Cinema hardly altered the street, since it was situated in an existing building. Its replacement had an elegant formal façade. Dent's monumental 1914 Grand Theatre towered above the street, but despite the considerable use of concrete, it used terracotta and brick for its main effect.

The introduction of the commercial postcard saw a boom after 1904 in pictorial views, Market and George Streets being the most photographed. Early postcard series were published locally by A.H. Weale of Victoria Road, the *Tamworth Herald* and printers Carricks of George Street, and Woodcock of Bolebridge Street. Others were published by national postcard firms such as Valentine's, Shaw and Knight.

The main public events photographed in the interwar years were the Duke of York's (later George VI) visit to Tamworth and the surrounding areas in 1924, and the popular annual Tamworth carnivals, with their numerous lorry- or horse-drawn floats, tableaux and accompanying carnival queens.

The economic brake of the two world wars and the 1930s Depression preserved Tamworth as a small nineteenth-century market town. The national economic revival and subsequent building and redevelopment booms following the Second World War saw a rapidly increasing rate of change. This began in the 1950s and '60s, with the building of extensive housing estates, the Lichfield Street tower blocks and the Middle Entry shopping centre. The latter gave the town the new St Editha's Square in front of the parish church.

This collection of photographs, most dating from before the 1960s, will I hope revive happy memories for many readers, while for others it will be a fascinating record of the past.

SECTION ONE

Church Street

Church Street formed the principal west–east thoroughfare of ancient Tamworth. Its northern side lay in Staffordshire and part of its southern side in Warwickshire. The junction with Lichfield Street was formerly called the Carrefour crossroads.

The western section from here to the church was called High Street in 1295, and by 1377 Churchestrete. Its eastern section, known as Butcher Street, housed the swine market. The south side of Church Street once contained some of Tamworth's most attractive timbered buildings, including Middle Entry and the Old Paregoric Shop.

The Tamworth Co-op's newly acquired emporium on the corner of Aldergate (left) and 1–4 Church Street, decorated possibly for the 1919 peace celebrations. Its previous owner, from about 1884 until 1917, had been Alfred Sadler & Co. Ltd. The arched window glazing above and full glazing below (since altered) shows off an elaborate display of tinned and boxed goods. The record dividend was then £12,935, a vast sum in those days. The Co-op purchased the adjoining buildings, on the right in June 1931.

An attentive crowd of Co-op members attend the 1932 inauguration of their new sweet and tobacco shop. The single-storey shop with its splendid Gibbs and Canning terracotta façade has since been replaced by the modern entrance and cash till section.

The entrance to the first Sir Robert Peel's Old School Yard, in use as a school before 1830. The old police house (left) was part of Tamworth's first police station. The original three cottages became two shops, Joseph Paxton's general store and Shipley's on the corner of Church Lane. All of these buildings were demolished in about 1952.

Fred Cole with three Daimler hearses outside St Editha's churchyard, *c.* 1926. The two rear cars (left) had sliding coffin platforms. Behind is Shipley's corner shop with its elaborate barge-boards and the Old School Yard cottages, Church Lane.

St Editha's Parish Church dominates the old Mercian capital of Tamworth. A Saxon church was associated with King Offa's palace, and it is known that a fire in 1345 swept away the Norman replacement. The present fourteenth-century Decorated church has a unique double-spiral staircase.

St Editha's interior, by E.B. Hamel, *c.* 1829. The wrought-iron chancel screen is attributed to Robert Bakewell, *c.* 1725. The surviving Romanesque arches once supported a central tower, and the wooden gallery and organ stood in front of the west tower.

The chancel, *c.* 1855. Here we see (left) the Ferrers Monument, a plain glazed east window with the gothic reredos of 1852 and a cast-iron heating stove. On the right is the fine eighteenth-century three-decker pulpit with its reading desk below and tester above. Most of these features were swept away in the modernization of the 1870s and '80s.

The Revd Brooke Lambert (centre) was a reforming vicar of Tamworth from 1872 to 1878. His example laid the foundations for Revd William MacGregor's (second left) 1878–87 programme of improvement to both church and town. Also depicted are the curates of the day, on the extreme left Revd Wray Hunt, second right his brother Revd Jerram Hunt, and on the extreme right Revd Henry Mosley.

The Revd J.H. Courtney Clarke and his bell-ringers on the aisle roof. Back row, left to right: A.J. Chaplin; brothers Charles and William Chapman (both carpenters); H. Chapman; J.W. Parker, the public health inspector. Middle row: ? Young, Co-op butcher; Arthur Marks, who worked at Skeys; J. Chatterton, chief of Tamworth's fire brigade; James Pratt, baker; Joseph Timms; Robert Brindley, postmaster of Leys post office. Front row: Horace Goostry, churchwarden and gents' outfitter; Revd J.H. Courtney Clarke, vicar of Tamworth 1895–1915; Albert Stuart, churchwarden.

The north porch and St Editha's Church choir, 1922–3. Among them are the churchwardens, Mr John Parker (extreme left) and Mr Albert Dain (extreme right). In the centre of the front row are curate Revd Bernard Hughes, the vicar, Revd Herbert Rosher and, right, curate Revd Percy Boulton. In the centre of the middle row is Mr Henry Rose, choirmaster, and on the extreme right Mr Robert Westbury, verger.

'The bells! The bells!' – here being removed by the Loughborough Bell Founders, John Taylor and Co., to be recast, in 1931–2. Churchwarden Mr G. Perry stands with Miss W.E. Chaplin (bell-ringer) and her father Mr H.W. Chaplin, verger. The churchyard still possessed its 1821 fine wrought-iron lamp, gates and railings. The magnificent cusped braces of the Paregoric Shop and its later jettied or projecting top storey dominates the background.

Church Street, looking west from Colehill. On the south side (left) the Co-op's main offices with its Victorian shop windows of 1897, MacGregor's Institute, Baths, and the Paregoric Shop are visible. On the north side (right) the churchyard, the Vergery, Mould's Yard and the Old Stone Cross public house can be seen.

Tamworth's Baptist Tabernacle: now the Art Centre, it was originally built as Tamworth's theatre. It became in turn a pig market, Sir Robert Peel's Gungate malthouse and in 1870 a chapel. This porch was added in 1908. Its minister (1907–18), Revd Donald Fraser (inset), was killed in France while serving as an army chaplain.

Church Street, south side. The Revd William MacGregor purchased the Church Street and Colehill corner site in 1884, and helped to found the Co-op movement in Tamworth. The two white-gabled cottages became early Co-op shops. In 1886 MacGregor built his institute (with the jettied gable and oriel window) and swimming baths (centre).

The swimming baths, early 1900s. MacGregor promoted 'muscular Christianity' and self-education for Tamworth youth. His football team trained with swimming practice at the baths and played football in them when they were drained.

The Old Paregoric Shop. The corner town house and early Co-op shop of two gabled cottages were demolished and a new Co-op headquarters (left) built in 1897. MacGregor's Baths and Institute (centre), was a Victorian essay in 'neighbourly good manners' to the older jettied Paregoric Shop next door (right). The latter's first floor shows medieval cusped braces dating from 1400–1450.

The tiny Paregoric Shop (right) was named after a patent medicine containing opium. It sold other remedies as well as bread and humble necessities. Glimpsed underneath the half-timbered archway in Marshal's Yard were six small tenements, all of which were demolished in the 1930s.

Church Street, College Lane corner, 1950s. The Co-op's single-storey drapery store replaced the Paregoric Shop in the 1930s. The tallest building was Moll Baxter's lodging house, later Pickett's. The dormered cottages in the centre belonged to the Ormes, and the bow-window is that of Pat Huskin, seller of horse liniment.

Church Street's medieval timbered buildings, long since demolished and replaced by St Editha's Square, make a charming picture here. In the centre was Miss Godfrey's leather shop, no. 45, with the yellow boot trade sign. The mock Tudor jettied no. 46 was William Bradley's butcher's shop, and behind the cyclist was Day and Bill's, milliners.

Tamworth's fifteenth-century Church Street Middle Entry. This was a tall jettied building whose upper gable commanded a front view of the churchyard and police station, with side windows facing in each direction along the length of Church Street. The building's roof sheltered several small cottages along its left-hand side. The Middle Entry, or alleyway, can be seen bottom right; it was a public footpath, made available to the townspeople by Lord Townshend in 1805 – a winding passageway through to the Market Street exit, also called Middle Entry, lying to the north of the Town Hall. No. 50 Church Street, The Wheatsheaf public house, is shown on the right with its illuminated sign and small glass-paned entrance. All these buildings were demolished in the 1950s to make way for the Middle Entry shopping centre.

Church Street, early 1960s. Carroll's Army Stores are seen, and then 52–52a Hunter's Yard Entry. No. 53, Machin's pickle shop, became Roy Arnold's barbers. No. 54, previously Rex Bartle (gents' outfitters), is photographed here as Bob Walters. No. 55 was Wm Hunter's and later the Co-op butchers.

Mr William Hunter, butcher, and Hunter's Yard, opposite the police station. Hunter's Yard was completely hidden from the road by no. 50, the Wheatsheaf, and no. 51, Carroll's Army Stores. The yard contained Mr Hunter's house (no. 52), a cottage (no. 52a), plus slaughterhouse, saddle-room, stalls, loose box, poultry cabin and a large shed for carts and vans.

SECTION TWO

Aldergate

Originally called Elregate in 1294, Aldergate was known as Ellergate by 1347 and as Eldergate by 1422. It retains a few fine well-proportioned town houses of the late eighteenth and nineteenth centuries.

Mrs Priscilla Reed, tobacconist and confectioner, stands outside her shop's attractive bow window (left) at 3 Aldergate, *c.* 1930. Mr Alfred Naylor, clockmaker and repairer, shared the same premises, hence the clock displayed in the right-hand window.

Aldergate, west side, southern end. Shown from the left are the Free Methodist Chapel of 1886, followed by nos 1–2, then Perks and Stevenson, hairdressers, no. 3, previously Mrs Reed's sweet shop, and no. 4 on the corner was Young's paper and joke shop. St John Street, south side, is on the right.

St John's Roman Catholic Church, *c.* 1911. Built for £220 in 1828–9 with the priest's house on the left, it was not licensed for marriages until 1837, well after Peel's Catholic Emancipation Act of 1829. Behind it is the Victorian church hall with Father Norris' memorial, sculpted by H. Mitchell.

The Co-op Society's busy carts and delivery vans fill Orchard Street, *c.* 1907. St John Street and churchyard are on the right, and the Co-op's main yard lay off Offa Street, also on the right. The Tamworth Board School in Hospital Street is at the far end of Orchard Street.

Displayed in St John Street is a train of immaculately turned out horse-drawn carriages, part of E.J. (Edward) Cole's undertaking and carriage hire business, *c.* 1905. St John's Church (which is off to the left) provided a suitable location for this advertisement photograph, with its Sunday services, funerary and church event trade.

Nos 5, 6 and 7, on the west side of Aldergate in the 1960s, when nos 6 and 7 (right) were occupied by Redfern and Edge, corn merchants. No. 7 was previously Johnson's garage. The *Tamworth Herald* offices are now on the site of nos 5–6.

John and George Johnson's garage, 7 Aldergate, *c.* 1912. They began with a small cyclemaking firm in College Lane. By 1900 they had moved to 7 Aldergate and up to 1912 advertised as 'cyclemakers and engineers'. As engineers they continued to manufacture their own cars, with a garage and repair business, into the 1930s.

Thomas Hames and Sons, coach builders and painters, at 10 Aldergate, *c.* 1926. Left to right: Caleb Hames, Sydney Hames, Harold Richards (carpenter), Tom Hames, the oldest brother and signwriter. The delivery van inside reads F. Baylis and Sons, Family Butchers, Wilnecote. The *Tamworth Herald* now occupies the site.

Bernard Hames stands in front of his father's house and office, at 10 Aldergate. Edward Wood's yellow and red butcher's van with a left-hand steering wheel is probably a 1919 Model T Ford. To the right, at no. 11, Dr Lowson's bay window can be seen.

An advertisement for Henry Young Mitchell, stonemason, *c.* 1912. His son Henry Charles Mitchell, stonemason, was a local historian and author, and honorary curator of Tamworth Castle Museum. Mitchell's premises at 31 Aldergate is now a betting shop.

Tamworth Co-op Fish and Poultry Shop, with its sparkling white-tiled interior, was 'licensed to deal in game', and is seen here decorated for the 1935 Jubilee of King George V. Now, with the shop front bricked up, the building still serves as a Co-op warehouse.

SECTION THREE

Corporation Street

Corporation Street was a new street created by late Victorian civic pride. Land initially purchased from the 1884 Sir Robert Peel estate sale was added to by public funds from Victoria's 1887 Jubilee Celebrations, enabling the purchase of the Hamel family home, which later became the municipal offices. The creation of Corporation Street's southern approach saw the demolition of buildings on Church Street, as well as Bradbury Square, in 1900.

St Editha's Church and cemetery, 1870–80. This is an early view of the Aldergate, Church Street and library area, before the building of Corporation Street. The central high brick wall of 1797 enclosed the medieval cemetery plus northern extension (left) of 1730, and north-eastern addition of 1797 (right). The Aldergate cemetery extension in the foreground is probably the 1851 gift of Miss Wolferstan of Tamworth Castle.

Corporation Street is dominated by Tamworth's Assembly Rooms (centre). Built in 1889, they became the new venue for large public meetings and theatricals, in place of Thomas Guy's Town Hall. The Aldergate cemetery extension (left) was railed in, and the Carnegie Library built in 1905. On the right, the Tamworth North Staffs Territorial Army Drill Hall was built in 1911.

Tamworth Territorials at home outside the Drill Hall, 1919–20. This faded postcard is thought to show Mayor Millington and men of the North Staffordshire Regiment.

The Carnegie Library and a hearse. E.J. Cole, founder of the Gungate undertaking firm, proudly sits on the graceful carriage-hearse. The driver's seat formed the glass-sided housing for a small child's coffin.

The Co-op Society's entry for the Tamworth Carnival displays Co-op products, advertising and packaging by young society members. The yard behind lies between the Carnegie Library and the Assembly Rooms. The area today forms a small car-park.

The Assembly Rooms, seen with Tamworth's volunteer fire brigade's extending ladder-cart on the left. The Assembly Rooms were built by public subscription to celebrate Queen Victoria's 1887 Jubilee and opened two years later. The superb prescriptive borough coat-of-arms with its two mermaid supporters had not been registered with the College of Heraldry, which is why they cannot be used with the modern coat-of-arms.

The old municipal offices were built originally as a high status town house, and occupied in the 1880s by the Hamel family. For a time it housed the subscription library and the Natural History and Archaeological Society's meeting rooms. Following the creation of Corporation Street the house became the municipal offices, and remained so until they moved to Marmion House in Lichfield Street, in 1980–81.

The Tamworth Millenary ox roast of 1913. This grassed area on the west side of Corporation Street lay to the south of the Drill Hall, opposite the Carnegie Centre. The public paid 3*d*, 6*d* or 9*d* for various sized portions of meat, or 1*s* for a full plate.

The 6th North Staffordshire Regimental Band, *c*. 1925–9. Led by Drum Major Harold Chandler, it included buglers Edward Mortimer (glimpsed between two drummers, back row, left) and Fred Thompson (second on the right), who were accompanied by side drummer Henry Wright (3rd row), the tallest soldier in the band.

In *c.* 1880 the Revd William MacGregor built the single-storey eight-bedded Cottage Hospital, to which a second storey was added by public subscription. In 1889 Mrs Hutton added the nurses' wing (far right). By 1905, the date of this picture, the hospital contained twenty-six beds.

Interior of the male ward. In 1924 two new wards, bringing the total number of beds to fifty, and a Memorial Hall, used by out-patients, had been added by public subscription in memory of Tamworth men killed in the First World War.

SECTION FOUR

Upper Gungate

The northern extension of Lower Gungate was originally called Stony Lane. Palmer described it as 'very dirty, irregular and narrow', 'with a very few poor scattered and thatched cottages'. By the 1820s it had been widened and new houses built. The nineteenth-century dwellings clustered at the southern end of Upper Gungate were swept away. The northern end contains substantial Victorian and Edwardian villas. Similar prosperous housing extended beyond The Hutton Fountain into the Comberford, Wigginton and Ashby Roads.

E.J. Cole, undertaker, with a glass hearse, on the west side of Gungate, *c.* 1910. Mrs Mary Cole ran the sweet shop (left), and her husband the funeral parlour (centre) and adjacent house and offices in the three-storey building (right). The latter survives, but Mr Cole demolished the right-hand side of the building in 1917 and built a new home and offices. His wall advertisement states that he was a postmaster and owner of the Golden Cup pub in Lower Gungate.

E.J. Cole, by this time an elderly man, with four of his vehicles. Behind the two Daimler saloons is the back of the wooden-bodied 'ambulance-cum-infectious diseases van', and behind that is an earlier saloon. Mr Cole is standing in front of Agnes Kendrick's hairdresser's shop, next door to L. and D. Hardy's florists and fruiterers, with his 1917 funeral parlour (now the Co-op) on the right.

The Dog Inn, Upper Gungate. Left to right: Joseph Henry Salt Sen., licensee, E.J. Cole, funeral director, and Henry Salt Jun. To the left were a row of cottages and on the right a malt-house.

The Dog Cottages were named after the adjacent public house. These nineteenth-century workers' cottages were photographed immediately before their demolition.

The Hutton Fountain, Upper Gungate junction. This well-loved local landmark was given by Mrs Hutton as a memorial to her husband in 1898. She was a generous benefactress to the town, giving land for the Aldergate cemetery extension and funding for the building of the Cottage Hospital.

St James' 'Spital' Chapel is situated between the Wigginton and Ashby Roads. Founded in 1274 by Sir Philip Marmion for the Premonstratensian Order, it became a hospital (hence 'Spital'), *c.* 1349. Spital House (in the background) was built in 1855 for Bishop Steere's St Alban's Guild, a religious community for men. This project was later abandoned.

The Burton brewer James Eadie's offices on the corner of Upper Gungate (left) and no. 1 Albert Road. Mr, Mrs and Miss Thom are standing in the centre with Messrs Carter and Cope with the drays on the right, *c.* 1895–1900.

SECTION FIVE

Lower Gungate

Lower Gungate was recorded as Gumpiyat in 1289 and Gumpigate in 1290. It was a divided street, with the old grammar school in the western part lying in Staffordshire, and the eastern side with Guy's almshouses in Warwickshire.

E.A. Phipson was a most accurate artist. His 1898–1903 water-colour labelled *Gungate* could apply to either Upper or Lower Gungate. The cottages superficially look like 9–11 Lower Gungate, now the Old Bell art shop. However, neither the half-timbered framing nor the neighbouring buildings or their replacements are compatible with those illustrated by Phipson. Two other alternative sites are suggested, assuming that the buildings Phipson illustrated were demolished soon after 1900, and replaced by Victorian or Edwardian brick buildings which may themselves have been demolished later. The most likely site in Lower Gungate would be to the south of the original Guy's Almshouses (page 44) to the right of the neighbouring buildings (shown on page 46), between the old courts nos 2 and 3, and the 1950s former post office. The site is now part of the Precinct shopping centre. If the half-timbered buildings stood in Upper Gungate, the most likely solution, then they may have been to the extreme right of E.J. Cole's buildings, shown on page 33, in which case the replacement buildings would be Cole's (and now the Co-op's) funeral parlour on page 34.

The original Prince of Wales, Lower Gungate, with publican Mr Edwin Ashwood. He had the old premises demolished and the present fine public house of the same name built in 1894.

Mr Edwin Godderidge Ashwood and his family at the rear of the old Prince of Wales, 1891. Left to right: Mrs Eliza Ashwood (née Whitehouse) with baby Agnes, Emily, Elizabeth, Hilda. In front are Herbert and the dog.

Nos 23–5 Lower Gungate. In 1872 William Lea Jun. was described as a grocer and tea dealer; between 1884 and 1912 as a grocer and draper at no. 18, then no. 25 Lower Gungate. Extensive alteration or the final demolition is in progress here, sometime before 1900.

William Lea poses with his family outside his smart rebuilt draper's premises, adjoining the grammar school, *c.* 1900–1914. This is now the Grape and Grain health food shop.

Queen Elizabeth's Free Grammar School was founded by the medieval Guild of St George, which the Tudors acquired in 1547. Elizabeth I refounded it in 1588. Hamel's engraving shows schoolmaster Antrobus' rebuilding of 1677–8 of a brick schoolroom with Ionic capitals.

The old grammar school site. A new grammar school on Ashby Road was built for £3,100 in 1867–8. The four dwellings shown here retained the earlier stone decorative capitals from the 1678 building. Modern shop-fronts were subsequently inserted.

The Golden Cup public house, *c.* 1910. At that time 27 Lower Gungate, it was later renumbered no. 35. E.J. Cole, its proprietor, was also the undertaker and postmaster. Immaculately dressed, he poses here for an advertisement with his elegant glass hearse.

The Bell Inn, demolished in the late 1960s, once stood on the north-west corner of Lower Gungate (left) where it joined the south side of Aldergate (right). The Bell Inn was the chief posting inn on the northern side of the borough.

Not the old Globe Inn as originally thought, but recently identified as the old Three Tuns, 13 Lichfield Street. E.J. Cole is photographed with his enclosed horse-drawn coach, and daughter, Mabel Mary Cole, with her friend Hilda. Mr Smith purchased the Globe from Thomas Bath in 1898 for £4,000, then demolished and completely rebuilt it in 1901.

The Globe Inn Rifle Club, photographed by A.H. Weale, 1921–2. The double doors open on to Gungate (east side). Seated, left to right: H. Tansey, A. Biddle, C. Pownell (vice-captain), Frank Godfrey (mayor), W. Helmore, G. Lakin, T. Brown. Standing: A. Osborne, E. Osborne, E. Ramsell, J. Tansey, F. Bryan, J. Lakin, W. Lakin.

John 'Jim' Kingslake's butcher's shop on the east side of Gungate, *c.* 1915. This was a thriving business with meat purchased from Burton market. Mr Kingslake stands fourth from the left with (fifth) Mr William Redfern, well known for his racehorse, Last Post.

No. 50, on the east side of Lower Gungate, on the northern corner of Spinning School Lane, was Griffiths Engineers' Forge and Castle Cycle Works. On the left is the oldest Griffiths partner; second left, Edwin Griffiths, tailor, and far right, Charles Booth Griffiths, all photographed with their first bicycle to be exported to South Africa, 1904–5.

The interior of Griffiths Castle Cycle Works, *c.* 1904–12. On the left is the older Mr Griffiths, while his younger brother Charles is third from the left. The scene shows a hive of engineering activity with an interesting motorized tricycle, motor bike and an expensive early motor car.

Thomas Guy's Almshouses, Lower Gungate, reputedly built on the St George's Guild Hall site in 1678 for seven poor women. In 1692 Guy added seven more rooms for men. He became MP for Tamworth in 1695, but lost the election of 1707 and, accusing Tamworthians of ingratitude, transferred his fortune to London to build Guy's Hospital.

Guy's Almshouses. The Gungate frontage (opposite lower left) was refaced in 1827. Here we see the garden at the rear, where the fourteen inmates could grow their vegetables, and (right) Guy's Spinning School Lane extension of 1692.

The original interior of Guy's Almshouses, dating from *c.* 1692–3. This was one of the fourteen rooms for individual poor men and women. Two other rooms held Rawlett's library. All sixteen rooms were swept away by the present almshouses, rebuilt in 1913.

This was an attractive Dutch-style gable-ended property to the south of Guy's Almshouses. The double doors led to the slaughterhouse of Sidney Doggrell (and later his son), butchers of 63 Church Street.

Spring Gardens were an L-shaped row of small terraced cottages curling round the south and east sides of Guy's Almshouses. This view shows the demolition of the south range (left) looking towards Gungate.

SECTION SIX

Colehill

Colehill was known in medieval times as Cross Street. At its northern junction with Church Street (then Butcher's Street) stood the town's stone cross. In 1516 the butchers were forbidden to sharpen their knives on the cross. Tamworth Co-op Society buildings now dominate the northern end of Colehill.

Seventeen-year-old Lilian Barter won the Dramatic Society's Fancy Dress Show second prize in Dordon School Hall, 1921. Her costume was an innovative idea, since the Co-op Society was the first firm in Tamworth to introduce bread wrappers.

E.B. Hamel's 1829 view of Colehill from the Church Street junction in 1829 shows a short wide street lined with Georgian town houses, since converted into shops. Today only the one with the four-pillared porch retains its original façade. The Larkin family built the house, on the extreme right, in 1805.

The Tamworth Co-op, 8 Colehill, celebrates George V's 1935 Jubilee. This building, on the extreme left in Hamel's print (above), became Thomas Argyle's Town Clerk's and Solicitor's residence from *c.* 1860 until his death in 1898.

The Spot on the Bolebridge Street corner with George Street (right), *c.* 1900. Mr Percy Millington (centre) stands outside his fruit shop selling 'Canary and Jamaica bananas'. This property is shown earlier as a jettied half-timbered building in Hamel's engraving (opposite).

Tamworth Co-op's headquarters of 1897 on Colehill and Church Street corner, photographed during the 1951 Festival of Britain. It replaced the eighteenth-century town house shown by Hamel (right-hand side of the top picture opposite) and the two gabled cottages (page 16). On the left was MacGregor's Vicarage, now part of the Co-op.

L. DODD, GENERAL DRAPER AND MILLINER,

Ladies' Underclothing and Baby Linen in Great Variety. The Newest Materials and Latest Patterns. : Hosiery Linen, Calicoes and Flannels.

COLEHILL and GEORGE STREET, TAMWORTH.

Miss Lucy Dodd's draper's shop, stood on the corner of George Street (left) with 1 Colehill, *c.* 1910. Mr Thomas Cooke introduced the new-fangled sewing machine into Tamworth at his first clothing manufactory here, in the early 1850s.

Colehill, looking north towards Tamworth theatre/Baptist Chapel, *c.* 1930. Perkins the chemist's premises can be seen mid-right with a selection of local doctors' and lawyers' motor cars and a Hovis horse-drawn cart of the period.

The former Unitarian minister's house, built by the Revd Mr Byng, dates from the 1730s or '40s. The archway led to the Unitarian Chapel before Victoria Road was built. Photographed here, *c.* 1920, Mr Thomas Perkin, the chemist and dentist, stands in his doorway, with his son Ted standing on the right.

The Colehill corner with Victoria Road, 1875. The corner shop and the two ancient cottages in Victoria Road were demolished before 1880, to be replaced by Heath's shop (see below). The three grandly ornamental town houses survived, later to serve as shops.

Colehill, the south-east end corner with Victoria Road, *c.* 1902. Thomas Heath and Son's shoe shop, established before 1884, is the focus of the corner. The same building, minus the large windows, later became the Britannia Assurance buildings.

SECTION SEVEN

George Street

George Street was formerly called Bullstake Street. The Bullstake stood with its bull-ring at the junction of Colehill with Bolebridge Street, for medieval bull-baiting. It was believed that baiting tenderized the flesh.

George Street, like Colehill in the eighteenth to early nineteenth centuries, was lined with elegant two- and three-storey town houses. The late nineteenth century saw much rebuilding and many older houses were converted into shops. This wide street soon became the most attractive of the major streets in the town.

Postmen and telegraph boys outside 2 George Street, Tamworth's post office. From about 1872 until after 1900 Richard Minor Wallis was the long-serving postmaster. No. 3, the draper's shop on the right was Samuel Soden's in the 1880s, in the 1890s George Bowen's, by 1900 Arthur Bayfield's and Maxstead's after 1912.

George Street, looking west from its eastern junction of Bolebridge Street, Victoria Road and Colehill, *c.* 1912. This view shows on the left no. 2, the post office; no. 3, Maxstead's drapers, no. 4, Griffin's, watchmakers, no. 5, Wm Jenson's, wine merchants, no. 6, James Cartlidge, clothier and no. 7, Frisbys' shoe shop. On the right, no. 37, Jack Marriott, clothiers, and Tamworth Borough cart collecting horse manure.

The same view but in the late 1930s or '40s. The major addition on the right is the Grand Cinema, built in 1914, topped by the statue holding the lamp. On the south side left were, no. 1, Dunn's footwear, no. 2, the post office and no. 3, Maxstead's, drapers. Parked in the centre is Facey's furniture lorry, with Taylors, Cash Chemists at no. 37 (right).

Upper George Street, *c.* 1904. On the left at no. 13 was Joseph Ignatius Emery, furniture dealer. Yarrows clothiers were at the top of George Street; their shops, nos 21 and 22, were demolished in 1920. Shown on the right is College Lane corner, with no. 28, George Coleman, chemist, then no. 29, Thomas Cope, tailor, followed by no. 30, George Griffin, watchmaker. At no. 31 was William Prime, ironmonger. On the extreme right was no. 31a, the premises of Thomas Carrick, framer and printer of this postcard.

George Street with increased traffic, 1930s. The Midland Bank, built in 1920, replaced Yarrows at the top of the street. On the far corner of College Lane, an earlier gabled shop was demolished and replaced by Woolworths, opposite Milo Turner, chemist, on the near corner, right. The George and Dragon had been renamed the George Inn since the turn of the century.

George Griffin, jeweller and watchmaker, at 4 George Street, is Tamworth's longest surviving family firm. Established in 1860, from 1880 until *c.* 1912 their shop was at no. 30, on the opposite side of the street. The Edwardian-style frontage has elaborate ironwork and fine glazing.

Joseph Wehrle, jeweller and watchmaker, 10a George Street, *c.* 1900. This is an impressive shop-front, with two external wall showcases and a packed display of jewellery. Joseph Wehrle appears in the 1900–1912 directories, and Lambert Wehrle as proprietor in 1932. The next building on the right was the Bricklayers' Arms.

No. 11, the original Bricklayers' Arms. In 1862 Joseph Paviour, a Gungate bricklayer, was landlord, naming it after his trade. This 1872 photograph shows its new publican, James William Pemberton, previously landlord of the Old Stone Cross. Some time after 1884 the early Bricklayers' Arms was demolished and replaced by the rebuilt public house and row of shops on the corner of Common Lane.

Thornburn's footwear shop, no. 16, and the Palace Theatre, decorated for the 1911 Coronation of George V. John Thornburn, an innovative entrepreneur, opened his shop before 1892 and added a warehouse by 1900. The firm manufactured boots and shoes in their Two Gates factory, which later became Reliant Cars, and ran Tamworth's first taxi service. Thornburn had opened the Palace Theatre in November 1910, for variety acts and early films.

Thornburn completely modernized the original Palace façade before introducing the 'talkies' in April 1932. The North Staffordshire Territorial Band promoted a First World War film. Partially hidden, to the right of Colonel Wolferstan (in civvies), is manager Mr Emery and, front right, commissionaire Mr Cotterrill.

Thornburn's old Palace continued showing films until the new Palace Cinema opened on Whit Monday, 10 June 1935. Its formal restrained frontage incorporating two tenanted shops looked deceptively small. It seated 1,410 and included a spacious crush hall with a large waiting lounge.

James Yarrow's 'General Clothiers, Outfitters, Hosiery and Glover' corner shop photographed before the First World War. Established by Albert Yarrow in 1858 at 21 George Street (left), by 1892, the family was able to add 22 Market Street (right). Yarrow's was demolished in 1920 and replaced by the Midland Bank (now the Halifax).

The top end of George Street, looking east, *c.* 1905. No. 22, on the left, was home to the Star Tea Co., grocers, and Eastman's, butchers. The pub, at this time known as the New Empire, had formerly been the Coffee Pot Inn and William Tait's Palace of Varieties. On the right was Thornburn's 'Boot Market' and Lloyds Bank.

This is the same view, taken *c.* 1940. On the left, no. 22, 'New' no longer, the pub was now just the Empire, and A. Frederick Bircher the licensee in 1932. No. 24 was Oliver Boonham's Oliver's Hotel between 1912 and 1932, and had previously belonged to William Logan, a wine and spirits dealer, from 1862 to 1900. On the right is Lloyds Bank with its present façade, then newcomer of 1936, Burton Tailoring, followed by the new Palace Cinema.

William Facey's household furniture store, 26 and 27 George Street, on the corner of College Lane, *c.* 1930. These premises, including the tiny tobacconist's shop, were purchased by Woolworths, who added their red and gold façade in 1933. They completely rebuilt the shop after the Second World War.

College Lane, *c.* 1950. On the west side the original row of small cottages was later converted into small workshops. On the left was Gessey and Bramley brass finishers' factory. Under its archway was K. Allen, bookmaker. Harry Nickells, painter and decorator, occupied the first cottage. The low single-storey building ending with double doors at its right end was the Hopwas Waterboard stores. Other businesses were Fretwell the jeweller and watch repairer and A. Smith, bookie. The brick gable (right) was Mrs Wakefield's boarding house in the early twentieth century. By the 1950s it had become Lesser's furniture store, behind which rises the octagonal steepleless stump of St Editha's tower. In 1862 the Fire Station House was in College Lane, but by 1884 it had moved to underneath the Town Hall arches.

The National School was built on the site of the Vicar's College House, in 1828–9. The Church of England's day and Sunday school with its porch of four pilasters (since removed) used Dr Bell's monitor system of education in its two classrooms, one for boys and the other for girls.

College Lane, Tamworth Board School Infants, with thirty-six pupils, *c.* 1892. C.E. Weale's photograph shows the school yard and the back of the classrooms. The headmistress was Miss Marion Hughes with 330 enrolled pupils. Fourth from the right in the front row is young Agnes Ashwood.

College Lane Sunday School with billeted wounded soldiers, 1914–18. The resident caretaker and nurse-in-charge was Mrs Ada Hillman, with her husband, Thomas, in civvies behind her. Their son Frederick stands to the left and daughter Mabel is seated on the left. Miss Hilda Justice, the daughter of the town crier, is seated at the front.

The eastern section of George Street, *c.* 1912. On the left the shops at no. 33, W. Hamblett, tobacconist, and no. 34, John Lea, tailor, can be seen. The third longer range of shops contained no. 35, Charles Dent and Son, painters and decorators. These buildings were demolished in 1914 with neighbouring no. 34, to build Dent's Grand Cinema.

The same view with horse and trap, 1920. On the north side (left) is no. 32, the George Inn, and no. 33, Hambletts; the Grand Theatre or Cinema occupied old nos 34–5. On the right, no. 9 was the Home and Colonial (front), and further along no. 7 was Frisby's shoes.

Charles H. Dent's Grand Cinematograph Theatre, built 1914–15. It certainly lived up to its title, completely dwarfing its neighbours. It was crowned by a Gibbs and Canning 7 ft statue of a classical muse representing 'the Arts'. She stood with her arms raised, originally supporting a spherical lamp. The statue was later purchased by the Biddle family and used as a garden ornament. It is now in the Castle Museum.

First World War veterans with the band, officers and army chaplain in front. On the south side (left) stood no. 6, Bradleys, clothiers, with a white blind; no. 7, Frisby's shoes; no. 9, Arthur Bray, fruiterer and no. 10, Hilton's shoes. Dean the tailor occupied Common Lane corner, with the old Palace Cinema beyond.

The Mayor's Parade, 1930s. The brass band leads the fire brigade, police and girl guides. Lucy Dodd's draper at 1 Colehill stands on the George Street north side corner. Next door, Needham's sign hides part of the building's superb Gibbs and Canning terracotta façade.

SECTION EIGHT

Market Street

Originally called Castle Street, the triangular street betrays its medieval market-place origins. The insertion of a Norman motte and bailey castle into the Saxon burgh's south-west quadrant created a market at the castle gates.

Medieval houses lined the north and east sides of the street. By Henry VIII's reign, the castle's decline and silting of the moat with soil and rubbish necessitated wooden pilings for the foundations of new houses on the south side of the street.

The Staffordshire and Warwickshire parts of the town had their separate Town Halls. Their single replacement was built by Thomas Guy in 1701.

Hamel's 1829 engraving shows late medieval, gabled cottages. Many had their wooden frames replaced or refaced in seventeenth–eighteenth-century brick. In the nineteenth century larger shops and the Provincial and Midland Banks made Market Street second only to George Street in importance.

Behind Prime Minister Sir Robert Peel's statue of 1852 are two late medieval, gable-ended cottage-shops, one of which is jettied. A later brick colonnaded shop with iron railings stands on the left. These buildings also appear in Hamel's 1829 engraving and the newspaper illustration of the 1852 unveiling of the Peel Monument (page 72).

Tamworth's first known post office stood on the corner of Market Street and Silver Street. This half-timbered building was propped up and in danger of falling down. It was demolished in 1807 for the western corner extension of the King's Arms, later renamed the Peel Arms (see below).

The original section, right, of the Peel Arms has a pillared porch and main entrance, itself probably blocking an earlier passageway similar to that of King Street. The left (western) corner extension of 1807 replaced the earlier post office. The building, apart from its façade, was demolished in 1994.

Frederick George Allton's grocery store at 5 Market Street, photographed in 1899. Allton was already established here and at no. 4 as a confectioner before 1892. He employed four young boys aged between ten and fourteen, and his well-stocked shop sold Chivers' preserves, Eiffel Tower lemonade, ginger punch, Danish butter and tinned sockeye salmon.

Lee, late Butler, ironmongers, 6 Market Street. This shows a 'polite' brick façade on a timber-framed building of *c.* 1695. Two crude nineteenth-century bay windows were added later. John Butler started his nailmaking, white metal (tin goods) and ironmonger's business, *c.* 1834.

Mrs Mary Butler was an ironmonger and tinplate worker, 1862–72. Her daughter, Harriet Butler, continued the business from 1884 until 1892. By 1900 John Lee had transformed Butler's business façade with the addition of the late Victorian fully glazed shop frontage, crowned by elegant ironwork above.

Lee's executors continued the business until the 1920s, when Coleman Brothers took over. This long-established firm of ironmongers gave individual service, sadly missed nowadays. Fortunately the building has been sensitively restored by the present owners, the Smith Brothers.

Tamworth Athletic Football Club, the first winners of the Tamworth Charity Cup, 1894, outside the Market Vaults. Players included Sam Proudman, Tom Lycett and George Hooper in the front row; Tom Smith, Tom Grimshaw and Harry Richardson in the middle row; Albert Wood, Harry Davis, Jack Cough, Andrew Wright and Tony Woodcock in the back row.

Etienne Hamel's illustration of the Town Hall and Market Street in 1829 with a variety of small-scale buildings, is full of old-world charm. The two gabled cottages, one with a barber's pole, and the adjacent low-roofed building were soon demolished. The fourth building on the left, with its five-columned arcade, survived until after the 1850s.

The unveiling of the monument to Prime Minister Sir Robert Peel, 2 p.m., 23 July 1852. Sculpted by Matthew Noble, the 8 ft bronze statue's inauguration was conducted by Sir Charles Mansfield Clarke, Queen Adelaide's physician, with the Town Council and local gentry in attendance.

Thomas Guy, founder of Guy's Hospital and Tamworth's MP, built a new Town Hall in 1701. Originally it was completely free-standing upon three arcades, each of six Ionic columns. Above, the single large council chamber was also used for plays and public assemblies. On the left is Brooks' glass-gabled arcade, *c.* 1900.

This view of the south side of Market Street, right, was probably photographed during the festivities for Queen Victoria's Diamond Jubilee. To the left of the Town Hall is the borough's extending ladder-cart. For many years the Merryweather horse-drawn fire engine was housed under the Town Hall.

George Fitelson's Bazaar with Miss Marion Bramall (right), *c.* 1920. Tamworth's early covered market, it held 1,500 people when used by the Salvation Army in 1892, and stretched almost to Church Street. In the 1900s it was Brooks' and by 1912 Fitelson's, becoming from about 1932 until the late 1950s Peacock's Arcade.

No. 16, The Staffordshire Yeoman, with (possibly) Tom Griffiths, who succeeded his father as licensee. The pub closed in 1913 and became Mrs E. Wheeldon's hardware and toy shop. It stood opposite the Town Hall, whose arches can be seen reflected in its windows.

Mr J.H. Johnson, standing left with his market stall, *c.* 1908. He sold haberdashery, mainly ribbons, buttons and laces. Later Mrs Wheeldon took over this stall as part of her hardware and toy business at no. 16, the ex-Staffordshire Yeoman pub.

No. 20, George Mason, grocers, *c.* 1935. The staff pose for a picture, with George Harvey (left) and assistant Sidney Hatton (fifth left). The upper part, also visible behind Johnson's market stall, was converted from a billiard hall into a factory making haversack webbing for the armed forces during the Second World War.

A grand civic parade, celebrating the 1911 coronation of George V, led by the police, with two mayoral mace-bearers, the vicar of Tamworth and the mayor, followed by aldermen and councillors. Photographed from the south side of the Town Hall, Wootton's Drapery, Goostry's men's outfitters and the Town Hall Vaults public house are clearly visible. Headwear was *de rigueur*.

Goostry, gents' outfitters (left) and the Town Hall Vaults. This public house was built directly on the medieval ruins of the late thirteenth-century castle gatehouse, using the latter and its medieval bridge arch as its beer cellars.

Tamworth Castle's archway to Market Street. John Robins, London auctioneer and the castle's owner from 1821 to 1831, built the small single-room upper lodge (now the Civic Society shop) and the top of the arch incorporating the earlier medieval gatehouse.

No. 26, Smith and Garlick, drapers, 1900. By 1912 they also occupied no. 27 as milliners, ladies' outfitters, dyers and cleaners, and carpet warehousemen. Their staff decorated the passage between the Town Hall Vaults and the castle gateway with Chinese lanterns for the 1913 Tamworth Millenary Celebrations.

Frederick George Allton, grocer, confectioner, and now fruiterer at no. 30, conveniently opposite his earlier shops at nos 4 and 5 on the other side of the street, *c.* 1912. No. 30 boasts superior gilt signwriting and elaborate running foliage ironwork above.

Alderman Alfred Dyer's confectioner's and baker's premises at 34 Market Street (south side) is the scene, *c.* 1900. His three grandsons, Llewelyn, Stanley and Kenneth, were sons of Herbert Dyer. The ladies may have been family members or employees.

SECTION NINE

The Holloway and Tamworth Castle

The eastern side of Silver Street and the Holloway still survives intact, together with Lady Bank on the Holloway's western side. The castle is approached through an attractive castle lodge, built in 1810.

The Castle Hotel and its proprietor, William Tempest. In 1862 Tempest was at the Peel Arms, headquarters of the Peel faction. By 1880 he had moved to the political opposition as tenant (and councillor) at the Castle Hotel. By 1884 Robert Griffin was proprietor and Tempest had moved to 125 Lichfield Street as a wine and spirit merchant, where he stayed until 1892, by which time he was an alderman and borough magistrate, residing at his Victorian villa of Mayfield House at Amington. This early photograph shows the Castle Hotel's horse-drawn luggage and passenger coach, for conveyance mainly from the railway station.

The Castle Hotel, *c.* 1908. The Castle was a premier coaching inn and former deadly rival to the Peel Arms opposite. Six maidservants perished in a disastrous fire on 2 November 1838. Architecturally the corner block is the oldest part, the centre block was built next and the ornate gabled section not until 1900.

The Holloway with little traffic, *c.* 1906. The castle's main entrance, Holloway Lodge, was built by the 2nd Marquess Townshend in 1810, as an archway separating two single-storey rooms. On purchase the Borough Council literally raised the roof and inserted an upper storey.

Hickson Brothers' luxury Guildford coach, 1932. This was a six-cylinder, ten miles to the gallon vehicle, and one of the first to have a separate driver's half-cab, with a charabanc-style canvas roll-back top. The Holloway was a popular pick-up point. Behind the coach is the Castle Bowling Club and the then Morgan's Brewery offices.

Tamworth Castle Bowling Club, ladies' evening, *c.* 1930. The building in the background, originally Lord Weymouth's town house, was never finished and eventually became Tamworth's workhouse. It is photographed here by A.H. Weale as Morgan's Brewery offices. Mr and Mrs F. Bills are in the centre of the front row, and Mr and Mrs Richards with Mr and Mrs W. Facey are on the extreme right.

Oliver Boonham (right) and Billy Smith (left) outside the former's 5 Silver Street Wine and Spirit Vaults, 1899. This is an earlier building with a late Victorian fine brick doorway insertion. By 1912 Boonham opened his hotel at 24 George Street.

Tamworth Castle. The motte's trees are severely pollarded, showing the late medieval heightening of the twelfth-century shell-keep (left). In the centre are the Tudor warder's lodge and Norman tower. The 2nd Marquess Townshend rebuilt the north wing, increasing the height of the shell-keep to the right, in 1807–11.

Captain Thomas Woodcock and Tamworth Volunteer Fire Brigade on parade, *c.* 1920. Their Merryweather steam fire engine was purchased in 1875, with a hose cart and fire-escape (extending ladder-cart). Only the horses and two men are missing.

Staff of Tamworth general post office, *c.* 1905. This may have been the occasion of distributing long service awards, with white-bearded Charles Bailey (centre) being the most deserving. The background provides a rare view of the Castle Mills from the castle grounds.

Ladybridge and the Castle Mills, *c.* 1872. In 1776 three corn mills and one fulling mill were all under one roof. The corn mills were worked by three separate water-wheels. The fulling mill had one wheel working two pairs of fuller hammers, and another wheel for calendering and printing cotton cloth. The Castle Mills were demolished in 1920.

Castle grounds and Castle Mills from the River Anker, photographed by C.E. Weale, *c.* 1885. The Cooke family was in residence. The castle grounds retained their late Regency landscaping before the erection of the bandstand and later flower beds of the twentieth century.

Widower Thomas Cooke and family, tenants of Tamworth Castle, *c.* 1870, outside the Holloway Lodge. Left to right: George (second son), Emma (oldest child), Thomas Cooke Sen., Albert (Fred), 'Lizzie', Annie, Frank, Thomas Cooke Jun. (oldest son and later mayor of Tamworth).

The ceremonial opening of Tamworth Castle as the borough's newly purchased museum by the Earl of Dartmouth (third left), 22 May 1899. Revd William MacGregor (fourth left) and Mayor Dr Sculthorpe promoted the castle's purchase from Lord Townshend for £3,000 to mark Queen Victoria's Diamond Jubilee.

The highlight of Tamworth's Millenary Celebrations was the civic unveiling of the castle's Aethelflaeda monument in 1913. Tamworth's mayoress, Mrs Harston, stands centre between the Earl and Countess Ferrers. Mayor Harston is partially hidden to the right of the countess.

Tamworth Borough Council at the ceremonial inauguration of Tamworth Castle in 1899. Front row, left to right: J. Coleman (macebearer), H. Hare, G. Hoskinson, Dr Sculthorpe (mayor), J. Matthews (town clerk), W. Tempest, T. Toplis (macebearer). Middle row: T. Richardson, A. Dyer, J.H. Dewes, C. Starkey, J. Dodd. Back row: S. Hardy, H.W. Sadler, T.W. Salt, A.J. Bartle, T. Luby, A. Brown.

The Masque of Tamworth, celebrating Queen Elizabeth I's 1560 Borough Charter, in the Great Hall, 1960. Front row, left to right: Elaine Price Evans (St Editha), Mabel Swift (Elizabeth I), Margaret Stevenson (St Editha). Back row: Selwyn Bate (Bishop), Harold Rhead (Sigthrigg), Stephen Farrow (King Athelstan), Arthur Windle or Archie Foote, Fred Swift (Narrator), Harry Baker, Mrs Chambers, June Sandland.

Tamworth Castle Great Hall, *c.* 1960. A visiting party of children admire a good old-fashioned display of arms and armour in the Great Hall.

The Castle's State Withdrawing-room, opulently furnished by multi-millionaire tenant Thomas Cooke for his family, and photographed here in the late 1880s or '90s. This large panelled room has a fine Jacobean fireplace and a superb heraldic frieze of the Ferrers, Compton and Shirley families' coats-of-arms.

SECTION TEN

Lichfield Street

Lichfield Street was one of Tamworth's longest streets. It was once densely populated with numerous courts, together with three additional streets: Brewery Lane, New Street and Peel Street. These together with the south-east corner properties were demolished around 1966, to make way for the high-rise flats and modern housing which now surrounds the architecturally important Elizabethan Moat House.

The White Lion Hotel, 127 Lichfield Street, *c.* 1927. Licensee Reuben Thompson stands at the main entrance. The corner angle doorway is often a Victorian feature. Thompson had previously been landlord of the Carpenters' Arms in Upper Gungate. He remained at the White Lion until its demolition in May 1935.

The White Horse Inn and south-east side of Lichfield Street (left) was opposite the rebuilt White Lion Hotel (right). Alas, the White Horse is no more; but this photograph was taken in February 1966 before demolition and the building of the Lichfield Street high-rise flats.

Nos 1–8 Old Lichfield Street await demolition, 1966. Its old courts and alleyways formed a close-knit community. The square entrance on the left led to Eaton's Yard, the semi-circular entrance in the centre to nos 5–8 and Mr Faulkner's milk-round yard. Polly's pet shop is on the right.

No. 8 Lichfield Street was once Harrison's butcher's shop, as can be seen in this 1920s picture. Mr Jim Kingslake returned to Tamworth after the First World War and purchased Harrison's business, retaining their name, and the superb royal coat-of-arms and wrought-iron lamp.

Polly's pet shop was previously Harrison's/Kingslake's butcher's shop. Lichfield Street widens at this point for an earlier market, possibly overlooked by the earlier Staffordshire Town Hall. The junctions of Old Brewery Lane and New Street with the Old Boot public house and Peel's Old School are on the right.

Morgan's Castle Brewery in Brewery Lane is seen here with its horses and carts, *c.* 1905. It lay behind Lord Weymouth's Workhouse and the present Castle Bowling Green.

Morgan's new chain-driven petrol lorry was probably an Albion, and is seen here *c.* 1920. On the left is Mr Wheeldon. Morgan's Brewery later became Gold and Wassalls, and was demolished to make way for the new Lichfield Street high-rise flats.

John O'Neil, butcher, of 106 Lichfield Street, sits centre in his white coat, surrounded by his friends and with his dog Spot at the rear of the Boot Inn, *c.* 1905. Standing behind him (hatless) are licensee John Ellson and his son of the same name.

Sir Robert Peel (2nd baronet) established this second Peel school in 1837, built in the 'Gothick' style on the south side of Lichfield Street. It replaced his father's earlier (1820) one-room school in the Old School Yard on the north side of Church Street.

Peel Street celebrates the end of the Second World War. This is a rare photograph of the street, which was probably mill-workers' housing and named after the 1st baronet, whose Lady Meadows Mill stood nearby.

The Moat House, *c.* 1880. This was a magnificent Tudor mansion with an outstanding Jacobean interior built by the Comberford family. For much of the nineteenth century it was a medical practice, and later a private lunatic asylum run by the Woody family.

Hildersheim House School, formerly of Lady Bank, on Lichfield Street, was a private school that stood on the present fire station married quarters' site. It is thought to have employed the German teachers that were fashionable before the First World War. In the 1930s it became Miss Shuttleworth's Ladies' School.

Tamworth's new fire station, which replaced Miss Shuttleworth's School, was opened in 1940. Front row, left to right: Peggy Perry, Jim Morris, Jim Radford (joint chief of the fire brigade and the waterworks), Fred Radford, Wesley Sharpe. Standing: Jeff Ford, Ken Wood, -?-, Dick Poole, 'Curley' Kennard, Reg Parnell, Wray Lester, Harry Wharmby, Bert Bullock. The dog was Patch.

Watercolour by E.V. Phipson, 1903. This range of cottages included courts nos 2 and 3 on the north side of Lichfield Street. The site of the cottage on the extreme left is now the middle of Wardle Street. The area from the half-timbered cottage to the three-storey house is the present forecourt of the Red Rose garage.

Thomas Cooke's clothing factory photographed by W. Hulland. As Cooke laconically recorded in his autobiography: 'On 10 November 1875, factory and all stock destroyed by fire. Damage nearly £18,000, fortunately insured . . . over 600 hands thus thrown out of employment. Rebuilt factory and resumed business.'

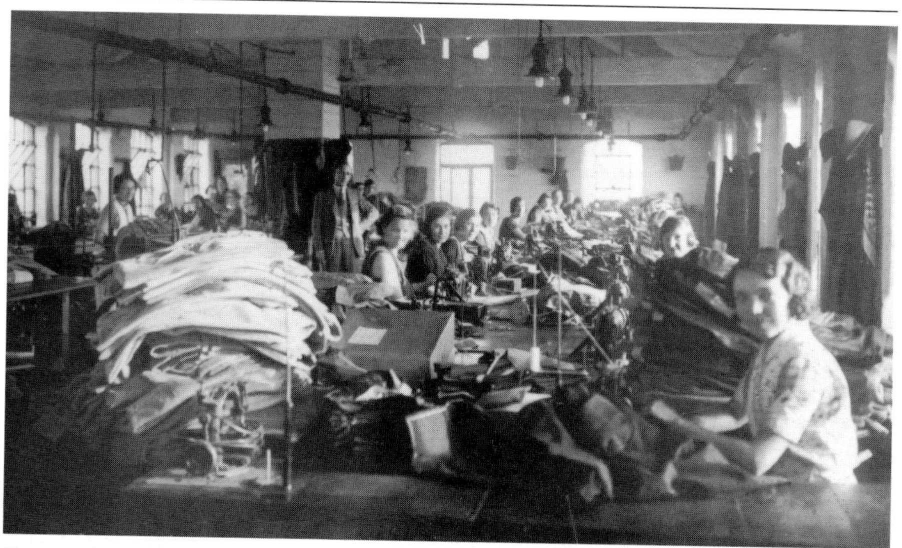

Shannon's purchased Cooke's factory before 1904. These are Shannon's workers in the 'top' or 'coat' room, photographed in 1920. On the left side of the work table are Mrs Bott, Gladys Plumbley, Nancy Bowler and Nancy Founds (?). On the right at the front are Miss Olive Perry and Mrs Cooper. In the centre is Mr Albert Coates.

Shannon's carnival float, with 'Miss Shannon', Dorothy Savage, and attendants. On the right-hand side are Josie Salt, Joan Shuttlebottom and Valerie Jackson, and on the left Lilian Finch, Doreen Everett and Cynthia Harper. The group of men are, left to right, manager Albert Coates, assistant manager Ken Chapman, the designer of the tableau John Tracey, and works mechanic and engineer Sid Ellis.

Sir Robert Peel (2nd baronet), the Prime Minister, had a red-brick school (left) built, *c.* 1850. It replaced Peel's smaller school on the opposite side of the street. The grand town house with its Venetian windows (right) is now the RAF Flarepath Club.

No. 110 (left) was once Taylor's bicycle repair shop. It became Dion's grocers in the 1920s or '30s and later Spenser's grocer-cum-sweet shop. No. 111, Watson's newsagents, photographed here in 1961, displays one of the last surviving jettied half-timbered façades, once a common feature of the town.

SECTION ELEVEN

Bolebridge Street

Bolebridge Street was originally called Bollebrugge Street after its medieval packhorse bridge. Until its recent demolition it was the longest street in Tamworth, initially a self-contained hamlet, lying beyond the walls of the town and stretching to Bolebridge and the River Anker.

The Jolly Button Turner Inn, Bolebridge Street, *c.* 1912. In 1818 Mr E. Pike was licensee and Elizabeth Pike the victualler. From 1834 until 1890 the Hastilow family were landlords, and by 1900 Mrs Ball and then her son George Ball (centre) were licensees until the early 1930s.

Old Bolebridge was built before 1316. It was a dog-leg narrow medieval bridge of twelve arches with triangular breakwaters built to carriageway level to provide refuge from traffic for pedestrians. Following a severe accident in 1820 the side walls were raised. The bridge was demolished in 1877.

The Bolebridge railway viaduct of the Birmingham to Derby Railway was officially opened on 4 August 1839 by George Stephenson driving his engine *Tamworth* over it. The medieval Bolebridge was replaced by the Victorian brick and iron bridge (1878–1935). This photograph dates from before the First World War.

Flooded Bolebridge Street's tall Bolebridge House stood at the south-west end of the earlier medieval bridge. Two cottages retained their close-studded timber-framed façade. The majority of children in this 1912 postcard are wearing stiff white collars and caps or hats.

The same buildings but looking north towards Hamel's Tape Mill and the Knob off to the right, 22 May 1932. The Knob was a triangular area which formed the eastern side of Mill Lane–Bolebridge Street. On the left, a pair of town houses were converted into shops by 1912. The second shop's façade is plated with huge enamelled commercial signs.

These were twelve terraced cottages called Arched Row, built behind the Red Lion and extending down to the River Anker. Their fireproof brick roof vaulting, or 'arches', were probably formed by re-using the semi-circular wooden construction frames from the canal.

The interior of the fireproof bedroom vaulting had exceptionally thick walls, best seen inside the window framing. Each cottage had two main rooms, one upstairs and one down, with an additional smaller bedroom. They were demolished in June 1953 by Mr Ben Paul.

The flooded middle section of Bolebridge Street, showing The Jolly Button Turner on the left, *c.* 1950s. No. 49, Bolebridge Cycles, was previously two houses, and the passageway led to a court of six houses. Hamel's Mill and the north end of the Knob is on the right.

Bolebridge Street's west side, looking south. Nos 58–62 were demolished in 1977. Here, cobbler Colin Seal cleans his shop front. At no. 57, Tudor House, was Mrs Rogers, clothes, and at no. 60, Renee Jackson, babywear. The entrance on the right led to Queen Street's terraced courtyard.

Tamworth Carnival, June 1975. A troupe of youngsters in bright yellow and dark blue uniforms march past Malkin's fruit and vegetable shop (left), N.J. Allen's sweet shop (previously Pearsalls) and Tom's Café, the former Old White Lion public house (right).

William Woodcock, at no. 85, started trading as a stationer and newsagent, but by 1900 had become a stationer and printer. Photographed here in 1912, Woodcock and Sons display their extensive range of postcards. Their printing works were here and in Heath Street.

'The Spot', a popular meeting-place on the corner of Bolebridge Street and George Street in the 1920s, '30s and '40s. In 1932 *Tamworth Mercury* offices (left) were shared with Woodcocks.

The Knob's southern end included Tamworth's ancient Tannery Yard. By the 1950s the tarmacked Knob provided parking outside Hamel's Mill's main gate.

Hamel's narrow tape Felix Mills had one of the longest histories of continuous manufacturing in Tamworth. The oldest part of the mill had an industrial cast-iron wall crane. The whole complex was replaced by the 'Bolebridge Egg' road development.

Felix Mills, Bolebridge Street (east side), showing the interior of the first-floor tape-packaging department, 1930s. In the centre tapes are being measured in 5 yd lengths by running the tapes up and over the rollers suspended from the ceiling.

SECTION TWELVE

Victoria Road

The building of the Birmingham and Derby Junction Railway in 1839 necessitated the creation of two new station approach roads to the town. Victoria and Albert Roads were named in honour of the royal visit of the queen and prince consort to Tamworth Drayton Manor in November 1843. Both roads are good examples of early Victorian town planning, tree-lined, wide and straight, with good substantial Victorian villas for the prosperous working and middle classes.

A Lilywhite postcard, *c.* 1922. Thomas Heath and Son's shoe shop stands on the Colehill and Victoria Road corner. Straight ahead is tree-lined Victoria Road, with a clear view of its southern side. Deeley and Sons, bakers and confectioners, are on the corner with Bolebridge Street.

Hickson Brothers' Crown garage, Victoria Road, *c.* 1934. Behind the newly built brick façade can be seen the ex-First World War metal Royal Flying Corps' aeroplane hangar, reassembled as a garage for Hicksons' luxury coaches.

Tamworth Co-op Society's Women's Guild proudly parade their banner in front of shops on the south side of Victoria Road, as they march towards the Marmion Street junction with Mill Lane, *c.* 1926.

Victoria Road's Unitarian Chapel was built in 1724, with a severe two-storey brick façade, stuccoed in modern times and with a later porch. This Nonconformist chapel was deliberately hidden behind other buildings, with the original entrance in Colehill (see page 51).

Looking across to the north side of Victoria Road, the premises (no. 3) of A. Colbourne, auctioneer and estate agent, are hidden by trees. Tamworthians watch the Co-op Society's horse-drawn floats pass by, *c.* 1926.

The Wesleyan Chapel from an early coloured postcard, published by the *Tamworth Herald, c.* 1904. Note the fine iron railings and Mr Rose's private garden (right), before the present extension to Marmion Street was built.

A large crowd congratulates Tamworth's new mayor, F.G. Allton, as he emerges from the Wesleyan Chapel, 1913. He broke with tradition by having the mayor-making religious ceremony held not in St Editha's Church, but in the Nonconformist chapel, to which he belonged.

Dr Sculthorpe, mayor of Tamworth (in 1894, 1895, 1898 and 1899) and his daughter Agnes outside his home, Victoria House (demolished and now the site of the telephone exchange), on the east side of Victoria Road. He promoted the Council's purchase of Tamworth Castle as a museum and campaigned vigorously for the vital improvement of Tamworth's water and sewage facilities.

Victoria Road's tree-lined centre section and railway station with, on the right, the cast-iron canopy of the Smith's, late Cheetam's, ginger beer and mineral water factory. The Albion Street corner shop (left) was once 1 Victoria Road, and was William Hulland, the engraver, artist and early Tamworth photographer's grocery during the 1870s and '80s.

Mr Richard's new Daimler, photographed outside Weale's studio, Victoria Road, *c.* 1912. Mr Richard was a wealthy small arms manufacturer in Soho, Birmingham. His home was Perrycrofts, Ashby Road, and his chauffeur-gardener and handyman, shown here, was a Mr Lee.

Victoria Road looking towards its distant junction with Marmion Street, *c.* 1932. Jewson's builder's yard now stands on the left, once the goods yard of the old Midland Railway. On the right stands the Tweeddale Arms public house.

SECTION THIRTEEN

Rail and Coal

Historically, Tamworth was a small market town served by toll roads. The introduction of the railways was accompanied by the rapid exploitation of local mining. It was the combination of these factors that led to a rapid growth of population and the expansion of Tamworth and the surrounding mining villages.

Miss Ida Holding, Midland Railway porter, photographed during the First World War. Her plain and simplified wartime uniform consisted of a broad-brimmed hat, blouse, tie, long skirt and heavy working boots. She married Jack Nicholas, who drove a railway horse and dray.

Prime Minister Peel promoted the building of the 'High Level' 1839 Birmingham to Derby, later the Midland Railway (top left), and then the 'Low Level' 1843 Trent Valley, the LNWR Railway (foreground). This woodcut shows the opening of the Trent Valley line and station on 4 December 1847. The architect was Mr Livock, whose richly ornamented station in his mock-Tudor-Jacobean style had a 135 ft façade and 300 ft long shallow platforms.

An Edwardian view of Tamworth station, showing the rich architectural detail of its elaborate gable-ends, tall decorative chimneys and pierced scrollwork. The forecourt bustles with a variety of interesting horse-drawn vehicles.

From December 1916 until 1919 the Tamworth Ladies Working League provided volunteers to run an overnight (8 p.m. to 4 a.m.) refreshment buffet on the LNWR platform for soldiers in transit during the First World War.

Employees of Hamel's George Street Bolebridge Mill, assembling in the Midland Railway's goods yard for the Tamworth Carnival. The brick goods building is an example of early railway architecture. Jewson's the builders merchants now occupy the site.

Amington Colliery 0–4–0 Bush saddle tank locomotive No. 1, *c.* 1910. On the footplate is the driver; centre, the salesman or 'outrider' of Birmingham Coal Exchange; right, the colliery engineer; front, shunter Mr Onions; centre, Mr Leedham and right, one of the company's largest shareholders.

A spectacular railway accident. The Midland Railway locomotive is concertinaed between the piled wreckage of the Amington and Glascote Colliery, SR and LMS wagons. This indicates a post-1928 to 1930s date for the accident.

Miners of Amington Colliery, with a private coal wagon belonging to the John Snow Company, Bristol, *c*. 1898. The two straw-bowlered gentlemen appear on the photograph opposite. Fourth from the left, aged only twelve or fourteen, is young miner Walter Oliver Perry.

Midland Railway 0–4–0 tank locomotive No. 1535 being raised by a steam crane following the accident shown opposite. Despite damage to its chimney and cab, it was repaired and returned to service.

Powerful diesel locomotives, Nos 10201 and 10202 of a class of three, ordered by Southern Railways but completed after nationalization, photographed passing through Polesworth station. Pooley Hall Colliery with its main office block is on the left; two mine-heads, aerial ropeways and spoil tips sprawl across the background.

Pooley Hall Colliery had its own railway and employed its own gangers or plate-layers. Here seven strong men are lifting a rail, *c.* 1952.

Pooley Hall Colliery had three attractive industrial 0–4–0 saddle tanks. The earliest, *Cowburn*, was built by Edwards in 1896. Driver Arthur Hudson is photographed here *c.* 1960, with *Kia-ora*, built in 1912, which like her later sister *Kapai* of 1920, was a Peckett loco.

Pooley Hall Colliery: an official inspection of miners by the then Duke of York (later George VI) accompanied by Colonel Chaytor, the mine owner, May 1924. In the background on the left is the North Warwickshire Mines Rescue lorry and two of the company's steam locomotives.

Miner Sydney Carter, third from the left, and four other members of the North Warwickshire Mines Rescue team, parade with their manager, Mr Watkins. Their specialized lorry is parked outside their Watling Street headquarters at Wilnecote, now the Commando Cleaning Company.

Hall End, Birch Coppice Colliery, in pre-nationalization days. On the left is the pithead to the 3 ft seam and on the right the pithead to the 5 ft seam. This colliery suffered a disastrous pit fire in 1910.

William Francis, Baddesley Colliery's famed 0–4–4–0 Beyer-Garratt locomotive of 1937, takes on water near the Midland Railway sidings. This was the third locomotive to be named after the son of the founder of the colliery, and is now preserved at Bressingham Gardens, at Diss, in Norfolk.

Tamworth (Alvecote) Colliery football team, supporters and officials. The team won the Lichfield, Wilnecote and Tamworth Charity and Tamworth Nursing Cups, and Trent Valley League Shield for the 1920/21 season.

Tamworth Colliery, renamed Alvecote Colliery after 1948, with its silted-up basin. The electricity generating turbine house and the screens to the main pithead are seen on the left. To the right are the smaller winding house and watershaft pithead. The boiler house is behind the colliery chimney.

Tamworth Colliery brickworks, photographed from the top of Tamworth Colliery's chimney, 1950s. They were directly linked by the bridge over the Coventry Canal. Tamworth Colliery brickyard is in the background.

Tamworth Colliery Brickworks and vertical boiler, late 1890s. Mr George Wilson, brickworker, stands on a loaded narrowboat on the Coventry Canal. Beyond are Tamworth Colliery's spoil mounds.

Brickmakers, Tamworth Colliery Brickworks Company, *c.* 1912. Among this mostly unidentified group are George Fielding, on the right of the front row; and second, third and fourth from the left in the middle row are Jack Shepherd, Edgar Wilson (foreman) and Isaac Baker.

Filling in the mine, Tamworth/Alvecote Colliery, *c.* 1950. Miners, left to right: Ernest Florendine, Ronny Geldard, Roy Moore, Jack Ealing, A. Smith, Eric Saddler, (Gil)'Bert' Wilson.

SECTION FOURTEEN

Canal and Coal

The old Borough of Tamworth refused to accommodate the new canal system within its borders. The first wave of industrial development during the Industrial Revolution thus took place along the Coventry Fazeley Canals, at Fazeley, Kettlebrook, Glascote and Amington.

A horse-drawn narrowboat loaded with coal is seen on the main Coventry Canal (right). The canal towpath bridge, left, crosses the entrance to Amington Basin, a small canal-rail trans-shipment wharf with its own short railway siding. The railway bridge, right, took Amington Colliery's coal through William H. Willday's coalyard (Glascote) into the Kettlebrook sidings.

Icebreaking on the Coventry Canal, Amington, *c.* 1960. This view from Hodge Lane canal bridge was photographed by Edgar Wilson. Butty boat *Branksome* brings up the rear of a second butty boat and two motor narrowboats.

Full steam ahead for a convoy of some ten narrowboats of Samuel E. Barlow's fleet, led by three motor boats. This was presumably also an icebreaking operation.

Samuel Barlow's Anchor Docks narrowboat repair and building yard, Glascote. Mr Andrew Penny, the yard's foreman for over forty years, stands on the stern of the *Hood*. Barlow's yard was famed for its decoration of painted roses.

British Waterways narrowboats awaiting orders, with *Evenlode* in the foreground, *c*. 1955. Behind and in the middle distance are Samuel Barlow's Anchor Docks, and beyond the Coventry Canal bridge at Glascote, the Anchor public house.

Five Thames lorries of Samuel Barlow's fleet are smartly turned out here. Barlow's fleet of over one hundred narrowboats was at its peak during the Second World War. He diversified into coal distribution by lorry in the 1950s.

Samuel Barlow Coal Company Ltd's brand new Ford Pilot van. Registration MOA 545, it was purchased from Beacon Motors Ltd for £814. Following an accident in 1954, it was repaired, registered as OOA 752 and sold in 1956 to Mr D. Hymer.

SECTION FIFTEEN

Other Industries

It was the exploitation of coal with the associated clay seams that saw the development of Gibbs and Canning at Glascote, and George Skeys at Wilnecote. Both became famous terracotta firms of national importance.

Death of an industry, July 1950. Messrs Gibbs and Canning's Glascote claypit, 240 ft deep, closed down after forty-six years, having yielded over 350,000 tons of clay. The number of clay miners employed since the 1870s had dropped from twenty to ten. Seen here are workmen Cyril Seabridge (second left) and standing mid-ladder (right), Les Proudman.

A giant caryatid, or half-draped architectural classical figure, over 12 ft tall, sculpted out of seven terracotta blocks by John Evans, Gibbs and Canning's chief modeller (right). He was assisted by Henry Stephenson (left) in August 1911. The figure was shipped to Vancouver.

Part of Gibbs and Canning's extensive workforce, 1928. This firm was one of the largest producers of architectural terracottas, and achieved international recognition for its decoration of the Royal Albert Hall and the South Kensington Natural Science Museum.

Gibbs and Canning's terracotta pipes are stacked in the workyard. In the background is a chimney, and one of their many kilns. Terracotta pipes, drains, sinks and domestic wares formed the bulk of their output.

A Gibbs and Canning lorry crammed with unglazed garden terracottas and a glazed white sink, as the firm's entry for the Tamworth Carnival, *c.* 1930.

Twelve mould-shop employees out of George Skeys' total of 600 workers. The women, including the Leedham sisters, all wear their best clothes and frilly aprons, deliberately hiding their laced-up boots or reinforced shoes.

Alder's Paper Mill works gang, *c.* 1890. A nicely posed formal photograph, with each workman carrying a tool representing his trade. This paper firm founded by Quakers and situated on the Lichfield Road continued in production for 200 years under various names.

Alder's paper mill and no. 2 papermaking machine, the calender and drying section, photographed in the 1920s or '30s.

Mill girls celebrate Christmas in Alder's paper bag department in the 1920s. The lattice-work framing to the main beams was a common feature in large-span industrial roofing of the period.

Bradley's Clothing Factory, Kettlebrook, *c.* 1927. Among the workers so far identified are sisters Norah and Nellie Twynum, Evelyn Pearn (née Bazeley), Dorothy 'Doll' Collins, Ida Butler, Lucy Towers, Winnie Bray, Dorothy Thompson, Flora Pearn and Elsie Pool.

Sixty-eight-year-old fitter, Jack Kinson, had completed fifty-five years service with Thompson and Southwick Ltd, Glascote, in 1950. He and his mate Wilf Wakelin inspect the firm's heavy cast-iron mine-head colliery winding pulleys.

SECTION SIXTEEN

Road Transport

Expensive motorized vehicles were a rare occurrence in Tamworth before 1914. A few early examples have already been illustrated.

Public transport led the way; horse-drawn brakes were slowly replaced by motorized buses. Private motoring grew slowly through the early 1920s, but did not make an impact until the late 1920s and early 1930s, when smaller cars at last became affordable for just over £100.

An unknown car and gentleman – no mechanic for, despite the overalls, he wears a stiff starched wing-collar. The missing registration may have been painted on the car's grille. The car was possibly newly delivered to a nearby garage and photographed outside the Castle Holloway Lodge, *c.* 1912.

Tamworth Oddfellows' day excursion at an unknown location. This is an early Midland charabanc with the fashionable but less common cigar or torpedo-shaped bodywork, unusually painted a light or white colour with gilt lettering but no lining. It was accompanied by a standard red-lined charabanc; see the opposite page.

The Aldergate Midland Bus Garage staff, mainly conductors and drivers, *c.* 1930. Front row: F. Smith, -?-, A. Willday, W. Blower, H. Cuffin, H. Brown, ? Kettle, T. Brammer, C.(H) Askell, -?-, -?-. Middle row: E. Crowley, -?-, F. Mundin, ? Carpenter, F. Spooner, T. Webb, N. Robinson, -?-, -?-, C. Pratt, A. Stanford, G. Smith. Back row: P. Shelton, S. Pownell, ? Williams, T. Neale, ? Sadler, -?-, T.(H) Elmore, S. James, ? Hornbuckle.

A pair of Midland charabancs (see left) are shown here parked in front of a late eighteenth- or early nineteenth-century hall, early 1920s. Among the gentlemen was probably Mr F. Godfrey of Church Street.

A nicely lined-out Midland bus, photographed in Polesworth Square, 1920s or '30s. The conductor, Mr Andy Stanford (on the left) was the son of Sergeant Joseph Stanford. His driver was Mr 'Bert' (Herbert) Carpenter.

A party of Lichfield Street neighbours, including the Cuffe, Edden and Ellard families, photographed at Matlock Bath, July 1925. The vehicle was one of the two Hickson brothers' 'Subsidy Dennis' charabancs, built on War Office surplus chassis left over from the First World War.

A Polesworth ladies' party outside the Abbey Gateway. The bus is Samuel Lathbury's new 1929 Glasgow Albion chassis. It had specialized bodywork by Wilsons of Perry Barr, with a reinforced floor of oak splats to cope with miners' boots. Lathbury's garage was behind the Town Hall Vaults public house in Market Street, Tamworth.

Proud new owner John C. Arnold, with driver's cap and greatcoat, stands in front of his new early model REO coach, complete with roof-rack and gleaming paintwork, *c.* 1926. His first Royal Blue luxury coach seated fourteen in relative comfort.

John Arnold's first Guildford half-cab thirty-two-seater coach. The driver was Mr Stanley Mayer, whose wife Margaret stands at the centre open window with Mrs John Arnold beside her on the right. Holding a child is Mrs Mayer's sister, and their mother Mrs White is standing on the extreme right. The seaside location is not known.

Eleven early motor bikes, three with sidecars, displayed outside Fidgeon's garage on the north-west corner of Fazeley Square, *c.* 1920. The car is probably a Ford. Fidgeon's branched out into the telephone installation and repair business between 1914 and 1925.

Tamworth Co-operative Society's aged lorry, its rear bodywork possibly made by its own carpentry department, *c.* 1930. Here it is displayed for one of the Tamworth parades. Its goods included HP bottles and packets of Ajax oats. The Co-op premises location is unidentified.

SECTION SEVENTEEN

Social and Village Life

The Castle's small photographic collection of personal, family, social and village life gives only a glimpse of the importance of the rich variety of social and sporting clubs, theatricals and carnivals, which made up the intensity of community life during the pre-TV age.

Sitting for a studio photograph was a social event often shared with relatives or friends. Here two Dorden miners, Messrs Douglas and Albrighton, sit before an elaborate late Victorian studio backcloth. This gives a positive air of affluence, somewhat removed from the harsh reality of everyday life in 1910.

'The Revels', a village celebration at Hall End Hall, 21 July 1910. A few mothers are strategically placed in the back row, with young girls and tiny tots in the front, all specially dressed alike with white bonnets.

A very smartly turned out Boys' Brigade with two clergymen present, *c.* 1900. To the right of the big drum is the Revd J.H. Courtney Clarke, vicar of Tamworth (1896–1915). The location is unknown.

The first Tamworth Girl Guides, White Rose Patrol, taking their child-nurse badge in the College Lane School Yard, *c.* 1928. Clockwise, from Joan Farley (seated left), Mabel Hall, Edna Purser, district commissioner (not named), Violet Crowe, Miss M. Lassetter (captain), Dorothy Wright, Letty Blanksby, Winifred Chaplin, Phyllis Belcher.

The Pageant of the Ages was written by A.H. Weale's daughter Margaret, and photographed in his Victoria Road studio, *c.* 1928. Back row, left to right: Eileen Hutchinson (seated), Jose Marriott, Mollie Richards, Margaret Weale, Nellie Moseley, Ivy Titterton, Beryl Tatton. Front row: Mirrie Bartle, Norma and Nancy Wilkins, Elsie Rutherford, Edith Perry, Muriel Whitehead (seated).

The Tamworth Carnival, with numerous floats and most large firms participating, was a popular entertainment raising money for charity. Gibbs and Canning employees formed the 'chain gang' with Mr Joe Ordish the first 'prisoner' on the left, 1930s. They were photographed in the Castle pleasure grounds.

Tamworth's Carnival Queen, Miss Donohoe and her attendants, July 1936. This stylish group photograph was taken by A.H. Weale in his studio garden at 23 Victoria Road.

The Revd William MacGregor (centre, back row) opened his St George's Club in 1886, 'for boys who had left school, for recreation and instruction'. At their 1892 Prestatyn camp are Henry F. Walker, third left, back row, and brothers Henry, William and Albert Stubbs, fourth, fifth and sixth in the middle row. Their sports included quoits and football.

High summer during the Edwardian age of elegance. Tamworth Tennis Club relaxes after a match on 12 August 1908. Two of the Emery sisters and their brother Hubert were present with two French visitors; the location is unknown.

The Queen Elizabeth Grammar School, Ashby Road and school cricket team, *c.* 1926. Standing: Stanley Bourne, ? Cavaner, ? Watkins, ? Lea, George Edwards, Stan Mitchell, -?-, ? Hewitt. Seated: Mr Warillow (sports master), ? Carter, ? Kitchingman, Burkitt Jun. Headmaster Frank Burkitt (1922–48). In front is Norman Whitehead.

The Drayton Manor 'Sunday' cricket team, the majority of whom also played for Tamworth, photographed at their Fazeley Deer Park grounds, *c.* 1935. Seated, left to right: Leon Cox, Sherle Godderidge, Harry Dolphin, Alan Beard, P. Kinson, Bob Jones, Sam Bourne. Standing: Jack Hawksworth (groundsman and umpire), Harold Brierley, Les Matthews, John Richards, Les Johnson, Herbert Andrews (secretary).

The Fazeley Swifts Football Club, winners here of the Tamworth and District League and the Atherstone Nursing Cups, 1894–5. Front row, left to right: W. Richardson, J. Evans, F. Barratt, E. Simpkins, T. Smith. Middle row: R. Evans, H. Simkins, E. Hough. Back row: W. Webster, J. Richardson, C. Cotterill, A. Wright, E. Cox, J. Smith (trainer).

Tamworth Wednesday Football Club played on Wednesday afternoons. Their members were shopkeepers and allied traders. Bowler-hatted Mr Edden stands in the back row, fourth from the right. On 2 January 1897 they drew 1–1 with Whittington Barracks Volunteers, and a week later they scored 2 against Lichfield Early Closers' 3.

Amington Rovers Football Club, 1903–4. Few of the players have been identified, but among those in the front row are second from the left, ? Archer and right, John Archer. Walter Perry is standing on the right of the back row.

Tamworth Castle Football Club displaying their 1909/10 season trophies: the Midland Daily Telegraph and Tamworth Charity cups. The participants were photographed by A.H. Weale in the grounds of Tamworth Castle. Front row, left to right: H. Hickin (secretary), G. Matthews, S. Whitehead, E. Morgan (president), H. Stephenson (captain), T. Lowe (mayor), A. Seal, T. Pointon, G. Hoskison (alderman). Middle row: J. Hopkins (assistant secretary), L. Smith, S. Wale, E. Shelton, J. Sadler, W. Smith, Councillor T.W. Woodcock (chairman), W. Pendray, J. Cuffe, O. Morris, A. Wright (trainer). Back row: G. Perks, G. Claridge, H. Bray, H. Selvester, D. Fox (vice-captain), S. Cuffe, J. Morris, F. Walker, M. White, D. Lathbury, Councillor H. Harston.

The Pretty Pigs, Amington, a well-known pub previously named The Repington Arms. It became the headquarters of the Amington Rovers Football Club, whose football field lay behind the pub to the right.

The quaint level-crossing and signal box at Amington, photographed before the track was quadrupled in 1901.

Glascote Road looking east, late nineteenth century. Glascote Cemetery Lodge was built in 1876, and its first superintendent was Mr Chaplin, who is standing on the left. Behind the children is the wall of the Glascote Infants School yard. On the right is Glascote Methodist Chapel.

A Glascote cottage interior. The stark room with its plain rough table, stool and chair was typical of millions of homes of the period. The Brain children's tableau 'What is a home without a Mother?' won a national photographic competition. Such interior views are rare.

Kettlebrook Road floods, probably May 1932. Floods always brought out the crowds. The house on the left on the Glascote Road, Bolebridge Viaduct corner still stands. The interesting range of industrial mill housing on the right was demolished long ago.

Mr Frederick Wharton, retired papermaker, sitting in his son Wilfred Leonard Wharton's bakers and grocers cart near their business premises of 28 Cross Street, Kettlebrook, *c.* 1911. Mr Wharton Senior was a founder member of the Kettlebrook Chapel. The congregation previously held their services under his yard's open archway. The young man on the left was injured in the First World War and later worked at the Palace Cinema.

Peel's Old Mill, Fazeley. Robert Peel (1st baronet) purchased, with Joseph Wilkes of Measham, the estates of Lord Weymouth, which they divided up between them *c.* 1790. Having helped to build the Coventry and Fazeley Canals, Peel built his first water-powered cotton mill here by 1791.

A postcard by A.W. Mills of Lichfield of the east side of The Square, Fazeley. In the foreground is a butcher's shop and Hollingshead's cobbler's shop, on the corner with Atherstone Street, is on the right. Lorenzo Brown, the White Lion's licensee, also ran a local horse-drawn cab business from a yard at the back.

Mill Lane, Fazeley, leading to Peel's Mill (see opposite), *c.* 1926. Peel's original range of stabling on the right had fireproof vaulting and brick ceilings to the downstairs rooms too. They later became twenty-four millworkers' cottages. The tall chapel on the right became an abattoir for Baylis' butcher's shop (side wall, left).

The ceremonial unveiling of Fazeley's War Memorial on Sunday 25 July 1920. Atherstone Street, part of Watling Street (the A5), is on the left. Behind the gleaming white memorial and its elegant early lamp can be seen Hollingshead's cobbler's shop on the north-east corner of Fazeley Square.

Staff outside the domestic offices at Drayton Manor, home of the Peel family. Included here are: the butler, Mrs Clempson the cook, Miss Clempson the parlour maid, gamekeeper Mr Beamall and Alfred Washington the carpenter. Mr V. Coulson, the chauffeur, stands in the back row on the left.

This is a postcard bearing the legend 'D Corps Cadets at Drayton Manor', dated 14 September 1917. Presumably the Peel family estate was used as an army training camp for new recruits. Tragically, most would not return from the slaughter on the Western Front.

Polesworth High Street, 1912. A comprehensive view showing thatched half-timbered cottages adjacent to the Nethersole School. The opposite side shows the half-timbered jettied Abbey Gatehouse, and in the foreground on the right is a range of buildings of which only the gabled Congregational Chapel remains today.

The Congregational Chapel, High Street, Polesworth, *c.* 1912. The painter, boy and diagonal ladder make an unusual informal element, counterbalancing the formal group photograph of the chapel congregation in the centre. The cottage, no. 8, with the attractive Venetian window, has long been demolished.

Messrs Deeming, father and son, stand in front of their Palace Cinema, Polesworth, accompanying their family and employees' 1922 outing to Matlock. They also owned the village bakery and shop. The owner-driver, Mr Bertram Hickson, is dwarfed by his magnificent open-touring, six-wheel Lancia luxury coach.

Mr Hames, wheelwright, coffin maker and undertaker, in his forge work yard, at the Retreat, Newton Regis, *c.* 1900. Mr Thomas Hames, on the right, presents his family, left to right: William Webster, employee and wife's cousin, daughters Hilda, Thirza and Rhoda, wife Ann and son Fred.

Two Gates villagers are photographed informally at Two Gates A5 crossroads, using the raised pavement as a platform. Mr George French, the coal haulier for Whateley Collieries stands right. His horse and cart was stabled at the rear of the nearby public house.

Belgrave Miners' Welfare Committee members celebrate their club's double triumph of winning both the Snooker and Cribbage Silver Cups, 1948. The latter, won three times in a row, became the 'Belgrave Cup'. Front row, left to right: Sid Pearsall (Steward), Billy Walker, Les Burdett, Wal Yates, Mark Aldridge, Tommy Pritchard, Sid Jones, Dorothy Pearsall (Stewardess). Back row: Ben Jones, Joe Lea, Joe Alldritt, Sid Jones, Ernie Marklew, Jim Faulkner, Bob Evans, Vic Owen, Tommy Jackson, Joe Asprey, Albert Walker.

A. Mills' postcard looking eastward down a traffic-free Watling Street, pre-1914. A glass and cast-iron porch protects the grocer's shop (left), later Harry Lester's. Further down was Edward Wood's butcher's shop. On the south side opposite is the Globe Inn.

Wilnecote's toll house stood on Watling Street's southern side at the bottom of Quarry Hill. Its projecting three-sided front gave a clear view in both directions up the A5. The vanished toll bar or gate was originally next to the front door.

A postcard view taken from the bottom of Quarry Hill, Wilnecote, looking eastwards up the hill, 1920s. The projecting front of the old toll house is probably hidden behind the houses on the right.

C.E. Weale's photograph from near the top of Quarry Hill shows the village of Wilnecote nestling in the valley below, *c.* 1887. The Toll House front projects into the road, bottom left. The bonneted lady and girls wear aprons, while the boys sport caps, a bowler and a straw hat, providing a certain rustic charm to this early scene.

Acknowledgements

I wish to thank all the many people for their kindness and generosity over the past thirty years in contributing their photographs to the Tamworth Castle Photographic Collection. I also wish to thank Tamworth Borough Council and curatorial staff, both past and present, for their cooperation, help and support and for the use of the Castle Collection.

In particular, for additional help and advice, I extend my thanks to the following individuals, collectors and institutions:

Mr A. Archer • Mrs E. Ballard • Mr P. Barber • Mrs D. Bates
Mrs N. Biddle • Mr S. Bourne • Mr H. Brereton • Mr W. Burdett
Mr H. Carpenter • Miss W. Chaplin • Mr A. Coates • Miss L. Dakin
Mrs O.E. Dale • Mrs V. Dewes • Mrs M. Dixon • Mr P. Edden
Mrs M. Edwards • Mr M. Faulkner • Mr L. French • Mrs Fryer
Mr R. Gausden • Mr C. Gibson • Mrs E. Gow • Mr Griffin • Mr I. de Hamel
Mrs D. Hames • Mrs P. Hatton • Mr R. Hickman • Mr K. Hickson
Mr R. Hughes • The Revd D. Juliano • Mr J. Kingslake • Mr B. Lathbury
Mrs C. Mann • Mr R. Meeson • Mr M. Morgan • Mr G. Morrell
Mr Mortimer • Mr S. Munn • Mrs C. Murphy • Mrs E. Newman-Smith
Mr D. Nickells • Mr J. Ordish • Mrs K. Parker • Miss O. Perry • Mrs J. Peters
Mr P. Pointon • Mrs Potts • Mr and Mrs J. Preston • Mrs G. Ritchie • Mr Salt
Mr P. Sandars • Mr and Mrs M. Siddals • Mr F. Shorthouse • Mr C. Smith
Mr B. Snow • Mr B. Spencer • Mrs H. Stevenson • Mrs J. Such
Mrs D. Sulima • Mrs M. Swift • Mr and Mrs J. Tracey • Mr J. Walsh
Mr J. Wheatley • Mr T. Wheeldon • Miss J. Wildig • Mr N. Winfield
Mrs C. Wood • Mrs P. Woodward • The Cooke Collection
Friends of Tamworth Castle Museum • The Gibson Collection
The Smith Brothers Collection • The Snow Collection • Tamworth Civic
Society • Tamworth Co-op Industrial Society • Tamworth Reference Library
The Weale Collection • The Wood Collection
Photography by Roger Hickman

The illustrations in this book are taken from the collections of Tamworth Castle Museum, which is owned and managed by Tamworth Borough Council. As well as an extensive photographic archive, the Castle Museum's collections include fine and decorative arts, rural and urban social history, archaeology, militaria, and period furniture on loan from the Victoria and Albert Museum.

Tamworth Castle Museum, The Holloway, Tamworth, Staffs B79 7LR